COSMIC ECSTASY

-Exploring the inner radiance

An Anthology of poems

-Ciju Jonathan

ISBN: 979-8-8676-6747-4

Table of Contents

Foreword

In the vast landscape of human expression, "Cosmic Ecstasy" stands as a poetic tapestry, woven with threads of spirituality, happiness, and profound insights. As a seasoned Psychotherapist, I approach these verses not merely as the words of an author, but as a witness to the transformative power embedded in every line.

At its core, this collection invites readers into a realm where spirituality is not confined to the narrow corridors of doctrine but expands into the boundless expanse of happiness. Ciju gracefully challenges the conventional boundaries of perception, offering a mirror through which readers can rediscover the overlooked facets of their own pursuit of joy.

The poems within these pages gently peel back the layers of our existence, revealing the subtle nuances that elude our attention in the hustle of daily life. In navigating the shallows of spirituality, Ciju deftly guides us toward the profound realization that happiness, that elusive treasure, is often hidden in plain sight, waiting to be noticed.

This compilation serves as a beacon for seekers, offering profound insights into the collective drift of our creation. Though the exploration may seem superficial on the surface, it serves as a foundation, a stepping stone inviting us to dive deeper into the reservoir of enlightenment.

Beyond the overarching theme of spirituality and happiness, "Cosmic Ecstasy" delicately touches upon the essence of femininity and the role of masculinity, all without disrupting the natural order. The author's words transcend the superficial, providing a thought-provoking exploration of the intricate dance between these fundamental forces.

As someone privileged to witness the author's personal and creative journey, I am struck by the remarkable maturity Ciju has attained. While as her husband, I may not have fully appreciated every nuance, as an author, she deserves not just applause but a resounding ovation for the depth and authenticity embedded in this collection.

This book is not merely a static creation; it is a marker of a journey, a testament to the author's evolution. It beckons us to anticipate more, promising a continuation of her creative odyssey. "Cosmic Ecstasy" is an offering, an exploration, and an invitation—a poetic voyage that invites us to rediscover the profound joy hidden in the cosmic dance of existence.

Jonathan Manoharadhas
Psychological Counsellor & Psychotherapist

Preface

I still wonder, what ignited the spark within me to weave these verses into existence. Yet, one thing is clear – I write with purpose and clarity. My journey into the world of poetry began when I was just a teenager, a different version of myself. Back then, my words were painted by the perceptions of adolescence. The ink flowed, the pages turned, and my first book came to life.

As the hands of time moved steadily forward, so did my mind. I've evolved and grown, seen the world through different lenses. Life has been my teacher, and experience, my guide. I find myself standing here as a new version of myself, with a mind that's broader and a perspective that's deeper. The decision to publish this collection wasn't driven by whim; it was fuelled by a desire to share my evolving thoughts, my soul's reflections. In these verses, you won't find a random anthology of poems; instead, you'll glimpse into my world, coloured with optimism and a deep appreciation for every facet of life. I choose not to keep these sentiments locked within; they're meant to be shared with you, my fellow travellers in this world.

Life is a continuous learning process, a journey of self-discovery. Every day, I uncover new truths, new joys, and new ways to embrace the world around me. I'm no sage claiming to know all of life's mysteries. Instead, I'm a curious wanderer, always seeking. My hope is that these words might change your perspective, encourage you to savour each moment, and appreciate the beauty of life.

This collection is a stark contrast to my first book, "*Humming Bliss - The Journey of Delight and Recovery*." That book was filled with pain, the echoes of suffering and other random themes. In "*Cosmic Ecstasy-Exploring the inner radiance*", you'll find the resonance of life in its many forms, the music of a soul that's found its melody.

I've come to understand that we are the sum of those we surround ourselves with. Jim Rohn's words ring true: "You're the average of the five people you spend the most time with." It's the lively, optimistic souls in my life who have filled me with positivity. I'm deeply thankful for my husband, Jonathan, his love, like my poetry, is a work of art in progress, always evolving, growing, and flourishing. With him, I've found not just a partner but a confidant, an ally, and the truest embodiment of love's enduring power. My heartfelt gratitude extends to my parents, who have showered me with endless love. Regardless of my age, they continue to see their little girl, and for that, I am truly thankful. If you are curious to know more about me, you'll find further insights at the end of this book in the 'About the Poet' section. While it may not reveal my entire story, it offers a glimpse into who I am and what fuels my creative journey.

Now, I invite you to dive into these verses. No need for a biography here. The words are ready, and I don't want to keep you waiting. Enjoy the cosmic journey that awaits within these pages.

Introduction

In the intricate tapestry of life, you find yourself traversing a labyrinth of experiences, seeking the elusive secret of happiness. With each step you take, you uncover the subtle mysteries that shape your joy, learning that it often dwells in the simplest moments and practices. In the first part of this collection, you embark on a journey to unravel the enigma of happiness, exploring the profound connection between your daily actions and the contentment you seek.

The second part invites you to delve into the realm of spiritual awakening, where the diverse values and beliefs of religions from all corners of the world unfold before your eyes. You celebrate the beauty in these values and gain a deeper understanding of the human connection that unites us all. Here, you also dive within, seeking the cosmic and eternal world that begins with self-awareness, urging you to explore the boundless inner cosmos.

The final part of this collection shifts its focus to consciousness and humanity, urging you to reflect upon your place in the contemporary world. In the minutiae of everyday life, you discover a wealth of lessons and contemplations. It encourages you to embrace different facets of your being, strive to embody the ideals of what it means to be truly human, and to live a life without the burden of regret.

Throughout this poetic journey, you explore themes that resonate with the human experience, spanning the mysteries of happiness, the depth of spirituality, and the essence of consciousness. A collection of 60 poems, each part paints a unique canvas, illuminating the multifaceted aspects of your existence. As you embark on this poetic voyage, may you find solace, inspiration, and a deeper connection to the tapestry of life that binds us all.

Part 1

The Hidden Key: Unravelling Happiness's Mystery

Cosmic Ecstasy

1. Celestial Wisdom

What do you grasp of stoic wisdom's grace?
The myriad paths that lead to life's embrace.
These treasures, hidden deep within our hearts,
Gift joy, love, and peace in life's countless parts.

Simple rules to guide through tempest's flight,
Control the self, in nature's bounds unite.
Embrace life's ebb and flow, the fleeting dance,
Find strength in trials, courage in every chance.

Seek virtue's path, in wisdom's light to grow,
Tame desires, let your inner strength flow.
Detach from judgments, cast by others' gaze,
For stoic journey's essence lies in self's own maze.

A voyage of self-discovery, profound and true,
In stoicism's embrace, find your own view.

2. Embracing Life's Little Wonders

In the darkest moments, when hope seems far,
Look up, find solace in the distant star.
A flicker in the vast celestial sea,
It whispers, "Dream, and you can be free."

Gratitude's the key to life's pure bliss,
The universe grants every gentle wish.
Place trust in God, the author of grace,
With patience, life's challenges we'll embrace.

Simple things, in truth, hold great import,
A child's smile, the simplest joys we court.
Nature's palette, blooms in vibrant array,
Leaves dancing, to the winds they obey.

In warm embraces, love's true essence lies,
It's all about the angle through which we see life's skies.
The choice is yours, perceive with an open heart,
These little things, a world of beauty they impart.

3. The path of passion

Career, a significant journey in life,
Not just a job, but a path we strive.
Seek out your passion, your heartfelt drive,
For therein lies the key to happiness rife.

Choosing a path solely for wealth's embrace,
May leave you yearning, without inner grace.
To Savor life's moments, to truly embrace,
Let love and passion, your career's base.

It's a choice not all may fully comprehend,
But for those who do, the message transcends.
In the arms of passion, our purpose amends,
A career built on love, where fulfilment descends.

An endeavour that sparks the fire within,
It's the place where you've always been keen.
A journey inspired by something unseen,
A career from the heart, where success convenes.
In the realm of passion, dreams take flight,
You'll find the strength to navigate any plight.
A career driven by what feels just right,
Is a treasure beyond measure, pure and bright.

So, seek your calling, let passion be your guide,
Let not mere money cause your dreams to hide.
For in the world of passion, you'll surely reside,
A career filled with love, where happiness presides.

4. The Flow of Life

In the grand tapestry of life's design,
We often ponder what lies in the signs,
Where are we headed, we sometimes ask,
Our journey's course, an intricate task.

But it's often wiser to simply let go,
With the currents of life, to ebb and to flow,
Forcing one's way, we may meet resistance,
While the universe decides with its persistence.

You'll find your desires in due time and place,
Patience is key, in life's intricate maze,
With gratitude, contentment, let your heart be filled,
As the universe's plan becomes beautifully revealed.

Life doesn't obey our beck and call,
It has its rhythm, it has its own thrall,
Trust in the power of the cosmic expanse,
If your wish is pure, it's given a chance.
And if what you seek doesn't instantly appear,
Don't be disheartened, don't let doubt steer,
For the universe, in its wisdom profound,
May have a different plan, a better ground.

Cosmic Ecstasy

Why chase what's not meant for your soul?
Let the universe's waves guide you toward your goal,
With belief in your heart, embrace the cosmic dance,
In its vast design, give life a chance.

It's the universe's art, like a masterpiece untold,
Guiding your journey, making your story unfold,
You'll reach your destination, this much is true,
With belief and trust, your dreams will come through.

5. Embracing Life's Challenges

In the grand theatre of existence, we find,
That every life has its ebb and its grind,
No one escapes the shadow of strife,
For hard times, they are a part of life.

Without the storms, how'd we know calm seas?
Hard times teach the heart to be at ease,
Life's classroom, a place of lessons profound,
In each challenge, wisdom's treasure can be found.

The trials we face, the struggles we endure,
They're not found in books, they're experiences pure,
Life's greatest lessons, we glean from strife,
They sculpt our character and shape our life.

Life isn't always a relentless, uphill climb,
It's in the little joys, in the rhythm and rhyme,
With a shift in perspective, the hard times will gleam,
A path of growth and a bridge to your dream.

For each day's a classroom, each challenge a chance,
To rise, to learn, and to enhance,
The tough roads we tread, they elevate,
Teaching us to cherish each moment, appreciate.

So, remember, hard times, they come and go,
In their wake, they leave what we need to grow,
Embrace each chapter, both sweet and rough,
For it's through the challenges that we find our stuff.

Let life's experiences be your guide,
To reach higher, to thrive, to take life in stride,
Each lesson learned, each hurdle climbed,
In hard times, the true beauty of life you'll find.

6. Celebrate Gratitude

In the depths of our hearts, it begins,

A feeling so pure, like the morning's first light,

Gratitude, the ember that warms us within,

Guiding us through day and into the night.

It's the stranger's small gesture, so often unseen,

A momentary kindness, a selfless endeavor,

A friend's open arms, where we've always been,

A bond that no distance can sever.

Life may sway like the ocean, unpredictable, wild,

People we meet, paths that may bend,

But through every twist, this truth reconciled,

Gratitude is the compass, a constant, true friend.

Yet sometimes, it's tested when arguments rise,

With those who've lent aid, now they stand opposed,

But remember the past, let resentments subside,

In gratitude's embrace, bitterness enclosed.

For even our enemies, those we can't hold dear,

Cosmic Ecstasy

Are part of life's tapestry, as strange as it seems,

In forgiving their faults and releasing our fear,

Our inner peace thrives, our spirits redeemed.

Gratitude, it's the gift you bestow on your soul,

A choice, ever-present, free to employ,

It mends what is broken, makes wounded hearts whole,

And brings inner serenity, a boundless, profound joy.

So, in every circumstance, let gratitude be,

The wellspring of calm in life's ebb and its flow,

With a heart full of thanks, you'll find yourself free,

As the architect of peace, where inner rivers of gratitude go.

7. Cultivate Positive Habits

In the realm of high-vibrational souls,
Where spiritual energies freely flow,
Resides a secret, not for the chosen few,
But for people like me and you.

The aura, a field beyond mere skin,
Holds treasures deep within.
Gratitude's the key, so pure and bright,
Expanding vessels, like radiant light.

Visualization, a canvas, blank and vast,
A life's portrait, in our hands at last.
A boundless power, waiting to be found,
In the art of feeling, on fertile ground.

But proceed with caution, there's a cost,
Higher vibes can be quickly lost.
Alcohol, though tempting it may be,
Disrupts the flow, impedes the free.

Cosmic Ecstasy

Embrace the shift, embrace the grace,
Visualize dreams in this endless space.
Avoid the toxins pulling you down,
Soon, you'll wear the higher vibe's crown.

Foster these habits, let your spirit rise,
On the path of high-vibration, reach the skies.

8. Unleashing Manifestation

In this world we navigate, both dark and fair,
Crafted by human hands, every joy, every care.
Harness the might within your very soul,
To become a beacon of goodness, your life's grand goal.

Don't let your mind wander, lost and untamed,
Forge your path, with your heart's fire, it's named.
The universe aligns to your soul's purest need,
It guides your steps, plant your heart's gentle seed.

For your greatest version to brightly unfurl,
Dive deep into life; let your spirit swirl.
Mind, body, emotions in harmonious connection,
Together orchestrate life's flawless direction.

Create a world of love and tranquil peace,
And your intentions and desires will increase.
Stay focused, aligned, let your energies flow,
Manifestation blooms where your intentions go.

One path, one purpose, with all your heart's might,
Will lead to your dreams, in the softest moonlight.
Manifest the reality you've long held inside,
In the universe's embrace, your desires will ride.

9. Simplicity's Embrace

In a world of complex, where worries tend to swarm,
Simplicity unveils life's true, tranquil form.
It sounds so easy, yet it holds the key,
To find joy in little things, be wild and free.

Each dawn's a purpose, a gift so pure,
Awaken with gratitude, that's the allure.
Eternal peace around, in nature's gentle grace,
Step out, explore, feel life's warm embrace.

Not within cold walls or concrete's hold,
But 'neath open skies, where stories are told.
Feel it within, and you'll surely find,
Life's simple treasures, in every moment, bind.

Simplicity, the secret to happiness's call,
In nature's loving arms, we find our all.
The world's a wondrous place, if we're willing to see,
The beauty in life's simplicity, forever to be.

10. Harmony in letting go

In life's tumultuous sea, stress can steer us astray,
Anxiety and depression may cloud our way.
Yet, hidden within, a secret mantra exists,
Simple and profound, a path to assist.

Humans, we are, control our endless quest,
But learning to let go is where we find rest.
Nature, the gentle caretaker of all,
Holds the key to peace within her thrall.

Let go of the pursuit of external delight,
For our striving generates anxiety's blight.
Shift your gaze, change your direction anew,
Embrace emptiness, and nature's course pursue.

Worry not excessively, relinquish your grip,
Release what you're holding, let your soul skip.
Learn the art of doing nothing, understand its grace,
In the hands of nature, let your being find its place.
Why burden yourself, battling the tides and the shore?
Emptiness and inaction are paths to explore.
Like a vacation midst life's endless demand,
Leave things alone, let solutions form like sands.

Cosmic Ecstasy

Life's complexities may seem like a curse,
But patience untangles, problems disperse.
In due time, all things will naturally align,
Embrace the journey, in the universe's design.

Abandon the race for fleeting happiness, dear friend,
It resides within, a treasure without an end.
Spare yourself from exhaustion, the endless chase,
Discover your essence, and inner peace you'll
embrace.

11. The Art of Wise Restraint

In the realm of words, have you heard the profound art,
Of selective silence, the wisdom it imparts?
Life's lessons, like treasures, some are meant to be concealed,
Shared only with those who may truly appreciate and yield.

We yearn to share our insights, to guide another's quest,
But not all hearts are open to what we suggest.
Some dreams, ambitions, burn like hidden stars,
To share them too soon could dim their potential to afar.

In this modern age of oversharing, it's true,
Everyone desires to unveil their life's view.
The choice is yours, whether to keep it hidden or show,
But remember, the essence of privacy has its own unique glow.

When we lay bare every aspect for the world to see,
We open ourselves to scrutiny and judgment, as you'll agree.
It's easy to complain of people's words unkind,
Yet, we must recognize, it's we who invited them in kind.

The power of selective silence, like an anchor strong,
Keeps you rooted; ensures you always belong.
So, choose what to share, what to keep in your heart,
In this harmonious balance, true strength shall impart.

12. Simplicity in a Complex World

In a world often labelled as complex, do we ever consider,
Who's behind the intricacies we encounter?
The truth is close at hand, no need to look too far,
It's us, the humans, who've raised the complexity bar.

Life's core, they claim, is inherently plain,
Yet, in our pursuit of progress, we've added strain.
We've crafted convenience in tangled threads,
As each person hurries like automaton spreads.

As robots emerge, some hearts are gripped by fear,
Afraid artificial intelligence will soon be here.
But cease the overthinking, quiet the inner storm,
We're meant to live in sync with nature's norm.

Once, we thrived in the wild, under nature's reign,
Revelling in the connection, it's hard to explain.
No company's offering can match its embrace,
Once you taste nature, it's a lifelong, cherished grace.

Cosmic Ecstasy

Cease the relentless race, take a mindful break,
Remember the times when family was our stake.
Yes, careers hold value, but let's comprehend,
In togetherness, life finds its blend.

Put a stop to the chase, stand still and observe,
In what the universe provides, we can preserve.
In tranquillity, your path will unravel and unfurl,
Trust that nature's embrace will secure and swirl.

13. The Delicate Art of Kindness

Are you one of the gentle souls,
Whose kindness endlessly flows?
This is for you, the kind at heart,
A gift of compassion, a work of art.

Kindness, a treasure, a precious boon,
But, dear heart, it's essential to attune.
There's a balance to be found,
In how your kindness should abound.

Understanding is the key, you see,
For everyone seeks something to be.
Yet, excessive kindness can sometimes fade,
Taken for granted, in the shadows, it's laid.

Be mindful of where your kindness falls,
Not all deserve your heartfelt calls.
Toxic souls, they might surround,
But your kindness, they don't truly confound.

They have lessons still to grasp,
In life's journey, they must clasp.
Change may come, or karma's twist,
So don't be worried by their mist.

Cosmic Ecstasy

Kindness is a balm, a soothing sound,
It uplifts the soul, makes hearts rebound.
Yet, choose wisely, where it's found,
For in the wrong hands, it can spin around.

To you, the kind and lovely heart,
Don't spread your kindness in every part.
Keep some secrets close and spare,
Your special showers, for those who truly care.

14. Wealth of Purpose

In a world where wealth is often deemed the prize,
Let's shift our focus, open our eyes.
Beyond financial success, a deeper truth unfurls,
The wealth of purpose and life's true pearls.

While money has its place in the modern scene,
True success is in realms more serene.
Earning the universe's blessings, understanding the whole,
Our connection to nature, each heart, and every soul.

Many chase the illusion of endless wealth,
But cease the race, discover your true self.
Channel your energies, where influence is your might,
Wealth in knowledge, a path shining bright.

You have a purpose, a unique role to play,
Yet some may obscure it, lead you astray.
Find your essence, let your spirit take flight,
Illuminate the world with your inner light.

Cosmic Ecstasy

Imagine a world where secrets are revealed,
No one's potential unjustly concealed.
It's aligning your life with a growth that's real,
Valuing personal evolution, a treasure to feel.

In this journey for purpose and inner wealth,
The riches of the soul far exceed material stealth.
Let your path be guided by a higher command,
Find fulfilment, embrace purpose, and take a stand.

15. Calm Within: Navigating Life's Currents

Observing life from a tranquil shore,
Grasping truth, understanding evermore.
Nature's calmness, a mirror to find,
Within us, let it peacefully bind.

In a world of instant reaction, so fast,
Give yourself a moment, let it last.
In response, your inner wisdom shines,
Preventing turmoil, breaking reactive lines.

Non-reactivity, not bottling up or hiding,
It's the art of response, in grace abiding.
Impulsiveness breeds negativity's cost,
The power to transcend it, in serenity embossed.

Hurtful words from others may sting,
But master your emotions, let your spirit sing.
Beneath every perspective, empathy takes flight,
Anchoring your strength, in forgiveness's light.
True power lies in composure when provoked,
Not in shouting, control, its grace evoked.
The weak may clash, but the wise find a way,
To nurture peace, let tranquillity hold sway.

Cosmic Ecstasy

Build a life harmonious, peaceful, and free,
Inspire others with your serene decree.
In calmness, lead, as others follow your cue,
In the gentle current, find a brighter view.

16. From Conflict to Cooperation

Adopt a flexible stance in the world's grand design,
Yet hold steadfast within, a balance so divine.
Many in this age yearn for contentment's embrace,
Acceptance is the key, finding one's place.

The universe's wisdom, a lesson profound,
The more we demand, the more we're unbound.
Refuse to be a mere puppet, tossed by the tide,
Embrace destiny, and peace will reside.

In the pursuit of desires, more we often seek,
Neglecting the universe's truth, wisdom unique.
Within yourself, discover contentment's true grace,
Accept others as they are, in life's intricate space.

Facing unpredictability along the way,
We're all human, meant to cooperate and convey.
In today's world, conflicts and protests may ensue,
Yet understanding our purpose is what we must
pursue.

Cosmic Ecstasy

Living with nature, cooperation's sweet song,
Within, find serenity, it's been there all along.
Spread harmony and peace, let compassion increase,
For violence only deepens woes, inner peace brings release.

17. Slowing Down in a Fast-Paced World

In a world that applauds speed, let me be clear,
Faster isn't always better, my dear.
With smartphones, we access the globe in our hand,
But have you ever slowed down to understand?

Life's pace may vary, interpretations diverse,
Some may oppose, some may converse.
In the midst of lifestyle's rapid race,
Living in a slower rhythm reveals grace.

Slowing down is an art, a beautiful way,
To enhance life's brilliance, come what may.
The need for speed doesn't always hold true,
In haste, precious moments often slip through.

Yes, efficiency speeds up tasks and goals,
But it can also take a toll on our souls.
So slow down, my friend, take a moment to see,
The world is here, while you're aging, be free.

Don't let life pass by in a whirlwind's dance,
Take time to appreciate every circumstance.
In the rush of life, amidst the daily grind,
Find joy in slowing down, peace of mind.

18. The Recipe for Family Togetherness

In the hustle and bustle of modern life, we find,
Our food has also evolved, leaving traditions behind.
From fruits to lentils, all now a hybrid's creation,
Processed, fast, in search of quick gratification.

Cooked meals, a relic of days gone by,
The new generation's choice, a quick 'buy and fry.'
Time to cook, scarce amidst our toil,
And during work, even a lunch break we can't spoil.

But what are we truly gaining from this frantic race?
We work ourselves weary, in this life's maze.
The company pays, but it's health we should save,
Old age won't be a refuge if our health we engrave.

Focus on well-being, on staying strong and sound,
Balance your meals, let health abound.
For a thousand vacations, to embrace nature's song,
You must be hale, for that journey is long.

Have you ever considered the joy of cooking a meal?
Instead of processed fare, or the phone's restaurant deal.
Take a breath, slow down, savor the art,
Cook and share, let it mend every heart.

Cosmic Ecstasy

How many still gather at the dining table, I inquire?
Is it a screen, a podcast, or a TV that you desire?
Shut it all out, and instead sit and talk,
With your loved ones, on a dining table, take a walk.

Share a meal, share stories, and laughter's embrace,
Spread love and happiness, in each other's grace.
At least one meal together, with family, at the core,
Nourish your bonds, let life's blessings pour.

19. The Echo of Narcissus

In the world of Greek mythology, a tale unfolds,
Of Narcissus, a man, and his story is told.
The name once trended, a label for those self-absorbed,
But its meaning was often skewed and ignored.

Narcissism, they said, is self-love's embrace,
Yet the tale of Narcissus reveals more to its case.
A handsome young man, his ego knew no bounds,
He spurned every maiden; his heart knew no bounds.

Even Echo, Artemis' favoured nymph, he turned away,
For he basked in his own beauty's radiant display.
Hera's spiteful curse on Echo was known to all,
She could only repeat the words she heard in her thrall.

But Echo, despite her fate, longed for Narcissus' heart,
She sought his love, playing her own part.
Yet, Narcissus remained ensnared in self-love's chain,
His rejection of Echo, a heartache and pain.

Nemesis, the goddess of chaos, heard the plea,
To show Narcissus the consequences of vanity.
And so, Narcissus met his reflection's gaze,
Mesmerized, he spent his final days.

Drinking from a pool, he longed for his own affection,
His self-love became his ultimate affliction.
Echo, from the shadows, watched his last farewell,
From where he once lay, a narcissus bloom did swell.

Imagine being so consumed by your own conceit,
That self-love leads to a fate so bittersweet.
From Narcissus, "narcissism" we now define,
A lesson learned from myth, for all of humankind.
So if you find echoes of Narcissus within your own soul,
Learn from his downfall, make kindness your goal.
Shift your love from self to others, set it free,
For in that act, true fulfilment you will see.

20. The Dance of Time

Time flows, swift as a fleeting dream,
Youthful days to adulthood's gleam.
Life's wonder lies in its ceaseless march,
A journey of growth, from light to dark.

Mentally and physically, we bloom and sway,
In life's intricate dance, we find our way.
Embracing change, accepting who we are,
Correcting past missteps, we reach for the stars.

Life's a simple art, though it may seem complex,
Vulnerability's strength, in this life's text.
Trust the path, even when it seems tough,
It forges resilience, making you strong enough.

Not just strength alone, it nurtures self-advocacy,
In life's grand design, it's the key to tenacity.
It's not a mere journey; it's a dance, a song,
A timeless rhythm, where we all belong.

Cosmic Ecstasy

Part 2

The Alchemy of Awakening: Rising in Spirit

21. The inner Alchemy

In the grand symphony of life, it's said and known,
Mental strength, a cornerstone, brightly shone.
Beyond appearances, beneath the skin's disguise,
It's the inner power that makes us strong and wise.

In tough situations, when challenges arise,
Mental strength is the beacon, the light that guides.
It shapes our words, our actions, and our grace,
In the complex dance of life, it finds its space.

Connected to IQ and emotional intelligence, it's true,
The trio intertwines, a harmonious debut.
With intellect sharp and emotions in control,
Mental fortitude strengthens, making us whole.

Not everyone may boast genius IQ or EQ's height,
But in balance and harmony, they find their light.
A mind that's sturdy, and emotions that flow,
Together they nurture the strength to glow.

Cosmic Ecstasy

And when the magic of the spiritual realm draws near,
Our inner star, radiant and clear.
The bond between mind, heart, and the divine,
Elevates mental strength, a brilliant, cosmic sign.

So embrace the power within, let it unfurl,
In the grand tapestry of existence, it's a precious pearl.
With intellect, emotion, and spirit's embrace,
We become the stars, guiding our own grace.

22. Threads of Faith

Spirituality, a silent art profound,
Within, its essence can be found.
In words, some aspects can be expressed,
Yet the deepest truths are felt, not guessed.

Guidance arises from our inner being,
Our core selves, the source of all seeing.
In a world of diverse beliefs and creed,
Common values weave a unity indeed.

Kindness, love, compassion's call,
Through various faiths, they stand tall.
Amidst debates and endless strife,
Embrace the essence of a harmonious life.

As I, an explorer of this spiritual quest,
Share the inspirations that I've been blessed.
In this vast world, I humbly learn and grow,
Uniting values from each faith's gentle flow.

23. Way of the Tao

Inner peace, a tranquil sea,
For those who follow Tao with glee.
Detachment, the core, where to commence,
In life's hustle and bustle, find your inner sense.

Nature's network, a tapestry so wide,
Life's questions answered in every stride.
Toss a stone, watch the ripples bloom,
But let it rest, they'll fade like a gentle plume.

Be like water, in Tao's warm embrace,
Face life's trials with unhurried grace.
Let things flow, don't put up a fight,
Inner peace returns, in its own soft light.

In this limitless cosmos, we each play a role,
A part of the whole, a fraction of the soul.
In tune with Tao, we find our place and key,
In its gentle wisdom, we're forever free.

24. The Inner Discipline

Self-discipline, a trait that defines your worth,
Setting you apart, a unique soul since birth.
Not from the worldly philosophers' say,
But within, you must find your own way.

Dreams, aspirations, in everyone reside,
Yet few embark on the journey with pride.
To make your dreams a tangible truth,
Self-discipline is the secret, the fountain of youth.

It's a spiritual path, this quest for more,
To grasp the world's spiritual core.
Self-discipline begins, not with just the frame,
But with a mind-body harmony, not the same.

The key to unlocking your desires, it seems,
Lies in embracing the path of your dreams.
With self-discipline, the journey unfolds,
In the spiritual reality, your story's told.

25. Beyond settling

In life, do you ever settle for less,
Or seek more, in the quest to progress?
Each day's a spiritual chapter, lessons anew,
Higher vibrations await, to reveal what's true.

Desires may linger, unmet and unfulfilled,
But failure's not the verdict, it's just a skill.
The universe whispers, "Don't settle for less,"
A spiritual path unfolds, in each soul's address.

Not the highest pinnacle, but a path unique,
To awaken the third eye, and new worlds seek.
See the universe through a different hue,
In your hands, with the cosmos, dreams come true.

Embrace the unknown, for it holds the key,
To discover the wonders that await thee.
In unsettled spirits, greatness finds its birth,
As you navigate life's journey, your own true worth.

26. The subconscious symphony

Connect with your higher self, embrace the truth within,
Feel the energies converge, where your journey begins.
Communication with your subconscious, an art of its own,
It holds powers untold, in the seeds that are sown.

Freud, Jung, their whispers of the subconscious mind,
But it speaks more than words, an infinite find.
Deep within, the answers to questions reside,
Listen to your inner self, let it be your guide.

In the depths of your being, a universe unfurls,
A map to self-discovery, as life's tapestry swirls.
Awaken the inner self, let its wisdom impart,
And find the answers you seek, in your very heart.

27. The Timeless Wisdom

Buddhism's values paint a way to exist,
In their simplicity, there's a profound twist.
Desire less, suffer not, the message so plain,
Contentment's the path, where true peace does reign.

In this ever-changing world, demands still increase,
Impermanence whispers, its wisdom and peace.
Pause, let desires abate, observe what's true,
Change how you respond, let your wisdom accrue.

Buddhism's well of inspiration, runs deep and wide,
Countless teachings, values, to be your guide.
A single poem's confines can't contain the vast sea,
But within its wisdom, your soul can roam free.

28. The Altruistic Heart

Altruism, a trait within our human core,
A drive to help, to give, to do more.
At times, even our own needs we'll deny,
To aid another, to ensure they can fly.

For in our hearts, it's a seed sown deep,
To give, to support, even when we're weak.
In moments of hunger, in moments of strife,
We share our sustenance, the essence of life.

Altruism, the opposite of selfish desire,
A flame of compassion, a selfless fire.
Debates may arise in the busy world's clamour,
But embrace the positives, let your heart be the
charmer.

In a world often driven by self-serving schemes,
Altruism shines bright in our collective dreams.
A testament to our shared humanity's grace,
As we lift one another in life's embrace.

29. Self-Discovery

Set your gaze inward, don't follow the crowd,
Life's a voyage within, where wisdom is found.
Amidst a sea of faces, unique and diverse,
Discover your essence, your path to traverse.

Why spend your days watching others afar,
Their stories distinct, like each shining star.
Life isn't a copy-paste, it's an uncharted trail,
A quest to unearth the secrets, hidden in your tale.

Curiosity in spirituality, a noble quest indeed,
But first, grasp your essence, let your spirit lead.
Know your deepest desires, who you aspire to be,
Embrace self-discovery, set your true self free.

In a world teeming with countless souls and dreams,
Live not for others, but for your inner streams.
For it's not in their shadows that your purpose lies,
But within, where your unique essence truly flies.

30. The Enduring Wisdom

In 600 pages and 114 chapters, a treasury lies,
Values of deep significance, where wisdom flies.
Kindness, a beacon that shines through the text,
Not just for people, but all life, it's complex.

Charity stands firm, a pillar of belief and grace,
A call to help and kindness in every place.
When harmed, forgiveness is the noble path,
Acceptance over anger, in the aftermath.

Patience, justice, and respect, they all implore,
Promises made with integrity, forevermore.
Anger's reward is meagre, it's often said,
In these profound values, let your soul be led.

The Quran's wisdom, a timeless source of light,
Guiding the heart through the day and night.

31. Guidance from Sikhism

In Sikhism's eternal light, we find our way,
Towards enlightenment, where values hold sway.
Generosity, honour, and honesty they impart,
A community of souls, with compassionate hearts.

Embracing a world beyond selfish desire,
In the realm of righteousness, they aspire.
Steering clear of vices that can lead astray,
From anger to lust, they tread a righteous way.

Stealing is forbidden, they firmly stand,
Earning with integrity, a principle so grand.
Exploitation they reject, with morals in sight,
Sikhism's teachings illuminate what's right.

Ignorance is banished, replaced by gratitude's song,
Daughters treasured; their lives strong.
Begging is shunned, self-sufficiency a creed,
Adultery they avoid, with unwavering heed.

With patience and self-control, they unite,
In Sikhism's embrace, their spirits take flight.
These are but glimpses of the values they hold,
In Sikhism's teachings, their stories unfold.

32. The Ancient Beliefs

In the tapestry of faith, diverse threads intertwine,
Hinduism's ancient wisdom, a beacon that does shine.
With no singular founder, it stands uniquely vast,
Flexible and profound, through the ages it does last.

Deities aplenty, yet one can be your guide,
A flexible devotion, in which beliefs reside.
The cycle of existence, birth, death, and rebirth,
Reincarnation's dance, across the vast Earth.

For karma, both good and bad, plays a crucial role,
In the grand scheme of life, it shapes the human soul.
A journey through eternity, a spiritual quest,
In Hinduism's embrace, we find our souls at rest.

Values of compassion, truth, and righteousness,
Dharma's moral code, in life's intricate chess.
Respect for all beings, a reverence for the Earth,
Hinduism's legacy, of immeasurable worth.

33. The Guiding Light

In Christianity's embrace, core values reside,
Love, unconditional, flows as an eternal tide.
Forgive and forget, the foundation we lay,
Release the past's burdens, let them fade away.

With open hearts, bitterness we dispel,
Forgiveness, the key to heal and make well.
Forgetting the wrongs, embracing anew,
Acceptance and love, in all that we do.

Hope, a constant companion, in each stride,
Belief in the unseen, where dreams abide.
Faith, a beacon, lighting the way,
Trust in the Divine, we fervently pray.

To receive God's blessings, humbly we ask,
In giving to others, we find our true task.
Helping our neighbours, in their times of need,
Christianity's values, in every deed.

34. Promises and Wisdom

In the depths of spirituality, secrets unfurl,
Revealing within us both moral and wisdom's pearl.
Morality, it speaks of promises we make,
A pledge, a commitment, not lightly to forsake.

To promise is to honour, a sacred bond we weave,
But wisdom whispers differently, in truths it does believe.
For the future's path is veiled, an uncertain, winding road,
Promises may become burdens, a heavy, cumbersome load.

The wise refrain from promises, the future's tale unknown,
They tread with cautious steps, in life's intricate zone.
Yet, let us not judge those whose words are firm and sure,
For morality and standards, their promises endure.

Respect those who uphold their word, their pledge intact,
But understand the weight they carry, a solemn, binding pact.
In wisdom's light, we learn, promises are not the key,
The future's veil they pierce, a truth that sets them free.

35.philosophical inquiry

"Who am I?" - a question profound and deep,
Unveiling the essence, our identities to keep.
Characteristics, values, beliefs intertwined,
In the mosaic of self, beautifully defined.

When we ponder others through a philosophical lens,
Individual's minds expand, wisdom transcends.
Reasoning, reflecting, their creativity flows,
Expressing their beliefs, a profound path it bestows.

With a thirst for knowledge, they're forever inspired,
Their minds and hearts, with wisdom, are wired.
In the quest of self and the world's diverse view,
Philosophy provides a compass, tried and true.

As they venture through this ever-changing domain,
They find identity is a complex, evolving terrain.
Every insight gained, every belief they collect,
Enhances their understanding, in every aspect.

In this exploration, they sow seeds of compassion,
Nurturing respect and empathy in every fashion.
For in the journey of self, and understanding others' plea,
Philosophy's guiding light shapes the people they will be.

36. The Veil of Perception

Perceptions shape the world we understand,
Where subjectivity and objectivity take their stand.
"Perception," a term that can mislead and obscure,
Our lives are like a real-time world, that's for sure.

But we're not just scientific models, cold and sterile,
Our existence is more than mere data in a file.
In philosophical debates, we ponder and we yearn,
Seeking truths about what we perceive and discern.

Colours, for instance, are they as they appear?
Or are they constructs, concepts we hold dear?
In the framework of direct realism, we reside,
Yet what we see may be just a mental ride.

Inferential realism offers a different view,
A perspective distinct from skepticism's crew.
It's a journey of understanding, not mere idealism,
A quest for truth that transcends perception's prism.

37. In Tune with Tao

In life's winding maze, we find our way,
Guided by Tao, both night and day.
A path as old as time, wisdom to share,
Embrace the journey, a gift so rare.

Tao's heart, a balance profound,
Yin and yang in harmony found.
The cosmic waltz, the universe's song,
Discover its secrets, where you belong.

Tao's not distant, it's close at hand,
Within life's flow, where we all stand.
Take your own steps, with purpose and grace,
Unearth the wisdom of this sacred place.

Unlock the universe's grand design,
Live in harmony, in nature's sign.
Tao's teachings beckon those who know,
With raised vibrations, their spirits glow.

38. In the Realm of Belief and Science

When diverse beliefs are the subject we explore,
Let's remember those who seek something more.
The ones with no God in their creed or scheme,
In science, they find their guiding beam.

Atheists they are, with a different creed,
To God's existence, they raise a question, indeed.
A speculative hypothesis, they perceive,
With low probabilities, they simply won't believe.

But do atheists, in science, truly reside?
Is it where their beliefs and thoughts coincide?
In the vast realm where belief and science convene,
Some embrace it fully, while others critique the scene.

Certain belief systems openly challenge and debate,
Science's influence and its authoritative state.
While others are eager to learn, understand, and discern,
Scientific knowledge, they passionately yearn.

Cosmic Ecstasy

In this ongoing debate, a complex display,
Beliefs and science entwine in a unique way.
Each individual on their distinct quest does embark,
Exploring knowledge and beliefs, where minds spark.

39. Inner Tranquillity

In the realm of beliefs and disbelief's sway,
From ancient wisdom's pages, we find our way.
But what elevates us to an ultimate plane,
Is meditation's gift, a tranquil domain.

A few moments of quiet, a portal it creates,
Embracing the world, as silence dictates.
Consider meditation, where serenity thrives,
An art of hush, where the spirit revives.

Submerge in the void, a tranquil expanse,
A state of emptiness, in a meditative dance.
When the true essence of meditation you glean,
It becomes an addicting, harmonious theme.

Peace becomes a constant, a cherished guide,
An addiction that nothing can truly hide.
Practice, practice, make it your daily devotion,
Till the art of meditation, a seamless emotion.

40. Awakening the spirit

Beyond our knowledge, a force unseen,
A creator or evolution, what's in between.
The question lingers, religion's role in view,
When kindness guides, what more must we pursue?

In days of old, battles waged in religion's name,
Now, amidst advancement and technology's flame.
If we still fight in the name of belief,
Our foundations falter, it's clear beyond belief.

The missing link in this intricate design,
A spiritual awakening, to align.
To strengthen the foundation, make it whole,
Awaken the spirit within every soul.

As we journey through life's intricate scheme,
Let love and compassion be our guiding beam.
In unity and understanding, we must believe,
A spiritual awakening, the way to peace we achieve.

Part 3

Explorations of Consciousness and Humanity: A Collection of Reflections

41. Embrace the Lifelong Learning

Never cease to learn, for life's a constant teacher,
Each day a new chapter, a valuable feature.
As I often proclaim, there's more to uncover,
In various forms, the essence of learning we rediscover.

Daily, we're students in the school of existence,
Challenging ourselves, breaking comfort's resistance.
An open spirit, ever ready to explore,
Diving into the depths, to gather knowledge galore.

For in the realm of wisdom, we find our true power,
The more we grasp, the higher we tower.
To halt the quest for knowledge is to cease to thrive,
Both in the tangible world and where our dreams come alive.

Our vast world and the web, like grand open halls,
Serve as boundless classrooms, where curiosity calls.
Every day, every way, new lessons unfold,
A lifetime of learning, a tale to be told.

42. Unveiling true feminism

Every human has the right to choose their way,
Equality for all, let injustice not hold sway.
One injustice breed another, we must break the chain,
Let's discuss feminism, with its principles to explain.

Feminism, it's not about opposing men's might,
But embracing women's strength in its purest light.
A celebration of beauty, strength, and grace,
For all genders, equal rights we must embrace.

In simple terms, it's about justice, fair and clear,
Respecting diverse experiences, drawing near.
Empowering women to reach their full potential,
Acknowledging their strengths, essential and essential.

In the modern era, views have shifted around,
Some think feminism means swapping roles, I've found.
But the heart of the matter remains steady and true,
Equality for all, for me, and for you.

Cosmic Ecstasy

Let's not pretend to be something we're not,
True feminism means fighting the battles we've got.
For justice and equality, we stand tall,
Embracing the rights and dignity of all.

43. The Sigma Male

Men are born with the innate drive to protect,
Yet not all who are male choose to reflect.
Only a few boys evolve into true men,
While others linger in a youthful den.

Let's delve into the sigma men, a unique breed,
Drawn to power, their nature and needs indeed.
How they wield it, both for good and ill,
Depends on character, an individual's skill.

In the realm of masculine energy, they reside,
Harnessing power to live life as their guide.
Power, it's not about control, it's true,
But the freedom to be, and to choose what you'll pursue.

In this world, men play a vital part,
Their support, a thread woven in life's art.
Whether direct or hidden, their strength we gain,
A testament to the power that shall ever remain.

44. The Shackles of Inadequacy

Deal with feelings of inferiority, they may persist,
Questioning your adequacy, that internal twist.
In a world where judgments and doubts abound,
Know that no one's perfect, let this truth resound.

To find belief within, let self-confidence bloom,
For if you don't trust yourself, you're left in gloom.
Assumptions and self-deception may play their part,
Release their hold, and reveal your inner heart.

Let go of facades, just be your true self,
With self-confidence and clarity on your shelf.
Clarity reveals life as it authentically stands,
No need for final answers, in its gentle hands.

Distinguish knowledge from clarity's clear sight,
Knowledge fixes, but clarity sheds the light.
In life, it's not the facts but how you perceive,
Clarity's the lens through which we truly believe.

45. The Epictetus philosophy

In history's pages, Epictetus' name is grand,
Beside Marcus Aurelius, they both stand.
A Stoic sage, their wisdom's profound,
Lessons in living, let their teachings resound.

In life's vast sea, this Stoic creed we find,
To differentiate what's in our grasp, in our mind.
Release the fret, for the unchangeable embrace,
Focus on our actions, let this wisdom retrace.

"Some things are in our control," he eloquently voiced,
Our thoughts, desires, what we've personally poised.
Yet release the grip on what lies beyond,
Body, property, reputation, let them respond.

Great leaders, not just in their speech,
But in their deeds, their lessons reach.
The path we tread, our choices displayed,
Live as we should, let actions cascade.

Cosmic Ecstasy

"Never call yourself a philosopher," he imparts,
Rather, let actions speak, follow Stoic arts.
Eat as you should, in humble attire,
Live your beliefs, let the world admire.

Habits, they hold us in their sway,
But Epictetus guides another way.
Set your principles, standards in your hand,
A character crafted, on life's stage to stand.

Prescribe to yourself a character, he insists,
Adhere to it closely, as your spirit persists.
With each small step, each day's endeavour,
Move closer to the you, you'd like to treasure.

46. The Bilingual Brain's Journey

A bilingual brain, a wondrous domain,
Learning languages, it's like mental terrain.
Thoughts in multiple tongues, a harmonious blend,
Exercising the mind, watch how it'll ascend.

Concentration sharpens, creativity takes flight,
Being bilingual bestows a radiant light.
Real-world implications, it's clear to see,
Great creativity unfolds, for you and me.

Cognitive reserve, a treasure to possess,
Building thinking abilities, no less.
Bilingual minds, swift in recovery,
Something special about language, in discovery.

Sounds, accents, and tones, a symphony profound,
In the brain's complex network, they resound.
Learning a new language, like a network anew,
Forging connections, strength it'll imbue.

The more languages you grasp, the more robust your mind,
A fortress of cognition, in any tongue, you'll find.

47. Prioritizing Your Well-Being and Aspirations

In life, there are some things you must hold dear,
Resist the urge to sacrifice them, have no fear.
For those who give all for loved ones' sake,
This message is for you, a stance to partake.

Put yourself first, live life by your design,
Focus on your mental health, let your star shine.
By safeguarding your well-being, without a compromise,
Both you and those around you will genuinely rise.

Your independence, a crucial facet of your existence,
Pursue your dreams, with unwavering persistence.
Never trade your aspirations for those who don't see,
The value of your goals, your spirit wild and free.

Financial stability, another vital part of the plan,
Earn your own, secure your future, lend a helping hand.
Remember, it's your strength that ensures their glee,
For family's happiness, set your own heart free.

If your priority's values and belief, protect them you must,
From sacrificing your all, in them, you place your trust.
Let your career be your passion, your path to chart,
Never relinquish it, follow the beat of your heart.

Hobbies and interests, let them thrive and soar,
Expressions of self, your soul they'll adore.
Though not all sacrifices should be declined,
Certain things you must never leave behind.

48. The Evolution of Understanding

In the realm of understanding, not all may see,
Teenagers embarking on their unique journey.
In this current phase of youth's whirlwind flight,
Let's refrain from imposing with all our might.

To the adults, a plea to pause and reflect,
Remember our own path, the steps we'd select.
The journey we've trodden, that's brought us here,
Transforming us, as we faced joy and fear.

Experience and learning, like treasures they unfold,
Accumulating wisdom, as life's stories are told.
From childhood's days, we gather bit by bit,
In our teenage years, believing we've got it.

But as teenagers grow, life's facets they explore,
Discovering perspectives, they hadn't known before.
True, not everyone will venture from their zone,
Yet those on the path to growth are not alone.

Blessed they are, the seekers of knowledge's grace,
Amassing wisdom, with each step they embrace.
For it's the journey that enriches, as we chart our way,
In the wealth of experience, clarity holds sway.

49. Living life free of regrets

Regrets, they burden, offer naught in return,
Mistakes, where lessons in life's pages we discern.
To stand where you are today, the path's been rough,
Strive for a life devoid of regrets, that's enough.

What's done, it's past, no power to rearrange,
Feel the emotions, don't fear the winds of change.
But holding on, it offers no solace, you see,
Be free, release the anchors, let yourself be.

Don't amass negativity, cast it aside,
No time for regrets, let that feeling subside.
Accept yourself, sinner and saint in each stride,
Correct, move forward, with nothing to hide.

Focus on your goodness, the light you bring,
In the essence of life, let your spirit take wing.
Regrets may visit, then depart, like a passing sea,
But the beauty of now, that's where you ought to be.

50. The Silent Plea of Nature

How can one assert that plants lack feelings, you ask,
Without solid evidence, it's a daunting task.
In this world, a realm of mystique and veiled clues,
Countless theories and truths, or perhaps none to choose.

In this enigmatic tapestry we call life,
Mysteries and narratives, a ceaseless rife.
Theories woven, like threads in the sky,
Yet truth or assumption, it's hard to descry.

While you're here, embrace life's vibrant array,
Harm no beings, let compassion hold sway.
Felling trees, dismissing their worth and grace,
For furniture or industry, is it a rightful chase?

Plants and trees, they're essential indeed,
In Earth's symphony, they help us all to feed.
Let's celebrate the existence of every small being,
For they're intertwined in the tapestry we're seeing.

Coexistence, not dominance, should be our creed,
For man's claim to superiority, we must take heed.
In the guise of being supreme, we disrupt the flow,

Cosmic Ecstasy

Unwittingly or knowingly, we deal nature a heavy blow.

As individuals, we may feel small and weak,
But collectively, we hold the power we seek.
Stand for ourselves, for all living things,
For the greater good, let harmony's song ring.

Will the world ever understand this plea we convey?
In unity and empathy, we can find a brighter day.

51. Perspectives on Gender

Gender, a topic for reflection,
As I grew up, it seemed simple, but now it's an intricate connection.
Today, parents raise their children without constraint,
Recognizing that gender's a personal preference, without complaint.

I concur with the idea of individual choice,
Yet why impose beliefs on others with a different voice?
If you ask me how many genders there may be,
I say two, but I respect diversity, you see.

For some, it's clear-cut, male and female they declare,
But others explore the spectrum, with identities to share.
In this world, there's a multitude of stories,
Of men, women, and those navigating diverse territories.

Abraham Lincoln once raised a question so profound,
'How many legs does a dog have when its tail's the extra round?'
The audience answered five, but Lincoln wisely stated,

Cosmic Ecstasy

'Calling it a leg doesn't make it so,' firmly he debated.

This tale serves as a reminder to our core,
In the absence of real issues, new debates we may explore,
So, let's stand firm in our beliefs and have our say,
For not endorsing 72 genders is our stance today.

52. The Weight of Our Wasted Abundance

In a world where food flows in abundance,
We're drowning in excess, a grievous occurrence.
We purchase with vigour, consume with delight,
Yet discard the surplus, heedless of the fight.

Have we ever considered, the sins that accrue,
When we squander the sustenance, without a clue?
There exist those who, with hunger's cruel pain,
Suffer silently, their plea unheard in vain.

Wasting food should be an act abhorred,
For others subsist on what we've ignored.
Across the globe, from every corner and place,
Some dine on our scraps, in a desperate race.

In towering supermarkets, aisles of plenty,
Goods laid waste, without conscience or empathy.
We're losing touch with food's intrinsic worth,
In our insatiable hunger for more since birth.

We must reflect on our choices, no delay,
The next time we waste, we should truly weigh,
The cost of abundance, the price of our sin,
And remember, to feed those in need is to win.

So, let's extend a hand to those who yearn,
Sharing our blessings, in kindness return.
Remember, when hunger strikes another's soul,
To offer a meal can make them whole.

53. The Genesis of Terrorism

Have you ever questioned how terror takes root,
Born from victimhood, where destinies are skewed?
A single soul, not solely at fault, it's true,
For hidden orchestrators, a darker hullabaloo.

But what compels this malevolence to sprout?
In a world where peace should be the ultimate route.
Could it be, the system's flawed, giving rise to despair,
And under a just system, peace would be everywhere?

If those who've suffered were nurtured and eased,
Kindness and empathy continually appeased,
Then messengers of peace would surely prevail,
In a world where harmony and love would never fail.

Remember, the blame falls not on individuals' shoulders,
But rather on the system, where conflict smoulders.
To obliterate this darkness, together we must strive,
Creating a world where peace can truly come alive.

54. Mind's Treasure Trove

The might of your mind, the strength of your thought,
Is the most potent force, in this world we've sought.
It's quite intriguing and often absurd to see,
How humanity values money more than wisdom's decree.

We're gifted knowledge, a divine endowment so grand,
To uplift our planet, together, hand in hand.
But in a world obsessed with monetary gain,
We often overlook the wisdom we could attain.

Why can't we share knowledge without asking for pay?
A billion-dollar question, it's clear as day.
In a world that soon shall transcend currency's flow,
True knowledge is the wealth that we should bestow.

You can teach and guide, help others grow,
But understanding is a personal journey we all must know.
Some things you can't impose, or force someone to see,
If they know, they know, for knowledge sets us free

55. The Authority Within and Parenting's Legacy

Authority and Authoritarianism, a distinct divide,
A true leader embodies the former, with grace they ride.
They don't dictate, but guide with a steady hand,
Taking responsibility and helping us understand.

In success, they share credit with the team,
In failure, they don't resort to a blame-filled scheme.
An authoritative leader shoulders the blame with care,
They protect the team, showing true leadership rare.

This approach extends to parenting, as we discern,
Permissive parents, in friendship, they yearn.
Boundaries forgotten, the child may lose their way,
Spoiled, they grow, with no rules to obey.

Neglectful parents, distant and uninvolved,
The child's development hardly resolved.
For children, what they see and hear does affect,
Their growth and behaviour, a path they reflect.

The roots of an individual's actions and thoughts,
Often trace back to childhood's tender spots.
A minute error in parenting, it's clear,
Can shape a person's life, even after many a year."

56. The Mirror of Imagination

Each of us, an internal narrative we hold,
Concealing the power within, stories untold.
Visualizing our goals, our minds have the might,
To turn dreams into reality, a wondrous sight.

Understanding this mechanism, we unlock the door,
To create a future from seeds we sow and explore.
A reality that mirrors our deepest desires, it's true,
Transforming aspirations, making dreams come through.

It's all about visualizing, believing, and then we achieve,
The Mirror Principle reflects what we perceive.
Not just an image, but ambitions so grand,
In a world where the mind shapes reality, we understand.

Visualization, the brush that paints our canvas wide,
Crafting vibrant images on life's adventurous ride.
Exploring endless possibilities, our minds unfurl,
Delving deep into the magic of thoughts, our world.

Cosmic Ecstasy

Envision, embark, and then experience the view,
Our thoughts and dreams shape what we pursue.
In the realm of our minds, stories take flight,
Crafting our destinies, painting our lives so bright.

57. Unseen Heroes

In a world of cinema, we find our source,
Following protagonists on a plotted course.
Actors play their roles, earning praise and gold,
While the true heroes' tales remain untold.

Do we fault humanity or society's way,
For not seeking knowledge they could convey?
Where does the crowd flock, what's our quest,
As we follow stars and neglect the rest?

A soldier on the screen, a far cry from the real,
In this world of illusion, our focus we conceal.
We relish the fake, but overlook the true,
Heroes among us, we often misconstrue.

We admire movie stars, what we wish to be,
Manifestations of desires we yearn to see.
Yet, the real heroes walk quietly, not seen,
Living with integrity in a world so keen.

In the most competitive land we reside,
Each one of us, with principles and conscience as our guide,
Is a silent hero, standing strong, taking a stand,
A beacon of light in a complex, demanding land.

58. The Quest for Ikigai

Ikigai, a Japanese treasure, a reason to be,
Where 'iki' is life, and 'gai' sets your worth free.
Your purpose, your joy, your daily inspiration,
It's what fuels your life with a deep dedication.

What you love, your passions so true,
What you excel in, what you were born to do.
Earning a living from your cherished skill,
And filling the world's needs, a purpose with goodwill.

Imagine your perfect day, from dawn till night,
This vision will guide you, shining your inner light.
Determining your ikigai, your truth so pure,
A path to walk on, a quest to endure.

The beauty of ikigai, what sets it apart,
Is the benefit to others, touching every heart.
Not just hedonic pleasure, but something more profound,
A life well-lived, true happiness is found.

Cosmic Ecstasy

It aligns with 'raison d'être,' the French proclaim,
And 'existensberättigande,' the Swedish name.
In Japan, it's believed, we all hold this key,
Our passion, talent, serving others, it's our destiny.

The journey may be long, self-exploration deep,
With reflections and time, your secrets to keep.
But you've got this, and the world will see,
A better place it becomes because of you and me.

59. The Oath of Power

In the pursuit of power, desires run deep,
Yet few are prepared the responsibility to keep.
This timeless adage, oft-repeated and wise,
Holds a truth that often belies.

Its origins reach back to ancient lore,
Philosophy's wisdom and texts of yore.
The saying proclaims a fundamental creed,
Of ethical obligation, we must heed.

"With great power comes great responsibility," it resounds,
A clarion call for those in power's bounds.
A pact to wield strength with prudence and care,
To weigh each decision, be it foul or fair.

This concept transcends the realm of capes and tights,
To leaders, to all in commanding heights.
From social influence to political might,
It demands actions that are just and right.

Power isn't a privilege for self-alone,
It's a burden shared, a duty to own.
An ethical compass for those who lead,
A solemn oath they must heed.

The phrase serves as a call to the mighty and strong,
To act ethically, to right what is wrong.
A reminder that power's not meant to exploit,
But to uplift, protect, and comfort and support.

60. The Cosmic Web

In the cosmic web, an intricate array,
Where every thread of existence holds sway.
Before our time, this connection was set,
Interwoven like the butterfly's flight, a cosmic roulette.

The concept of all things being interlinked and intertwined,
A profound notion in human thought enshrined.
From tiny particles to galaxies so grand,
In a web of unity, they're bound by an invisible hand.

The butterfly effect, chaos theory's famous guide,
Reveals how small changes can the future decide.
A wing's whisper in a faraway land,
Sets in motion events, profound and unplanned.

In nature's realm, ecosystems beautifully blend,
Where each life form on the other depends.
Sunlight feeds the plants, the animals feed,
A circle of life where no one's greed.

Cosmic Ecstasy

In human actions and choices, we hold the key,
To shape the world, both near and far, you see.
Our consumption, travel, and social accord,
Can impact society, for better or discord.

Conversely, acts of kindness, compassion's warm embrace,
Can trigger positive change, a ripple's graceful trace.
In the web of thoughts, feelings, and more,
Our emotions and actions an intricate rapport.

Recognizing this interconnected symphony,
We're called to share in a collective responsibility.
To move beyond self, embrace the greater whole,
A path to harmony, a more unified goal.

In sum, the belief in universal connection weaves,
A tapestry of life where everything conceives.
A call for a change in how we perceive,
To honour our ties, and in unity believe.

About the Poet

Ciju a spirited and joyful soul, finds immense delight in the simple things life has to offer. Her heart resonates with the beauty of the wilderness, and she is most at peace when wandering through the embrace of nature.

Whenever inspiration sparks within her, she weaves her thoughts and emotions into poetry, painting vivid landscapes of the soul. Her connection with the written word is a reflection of her innermost self.

Ciju is not just a poet; she's a seeker of knowledge. She dedicates herself to exploring the rich tapestry of world religions, drawing inspiration from the profound spiritualism that unites humanity. Her journey is one of continuous learning and introspection.

Nestled in the charming city of Sheffield, UK, she has found her second home, a place where her heart truly belongs. In her professional life, she is a listener, a patient and compassionate presence. Yet, when she returns to the sanctuary of her home, she transforms into a non-stop chat box, weaving laughter and love into every moment with her family, whom she holds dear above all else.

Ciju is a free-spirited, contented soul, guided by her passions and interests. She soars like a joyful bird, embracing the boundless world around her, and in turn, she continues to learn and grow. Her life is a testament to gratitude, cherishing the abundance the universe bestows upon her. In her contentment, she discovers the richest treasures life has to offer.

Contact information

Gmail: *ciju.silpa@gmail.com*

Acknowledgement

I would like to express my deep gratitude to my husband, Jonathan, who has been my unwavering support and my guiding light, always lifting my spirits to soar to new heights. His genuine admiration and joy in my success illuminate my path, and I am immensely grateful for his presence in my life.

I also want to extend my heartfelt appreciation to my parents, who have consistently believed in me and provided unwavering encouragement to excel in all aspects of life. Their trust and support have been instrumental in my journey.

To all my wonderful friends and family, I am truly thankful for your love, encouragement, and unwavering belief in my creative endeavours. Your presence in my life is a cherished blessing that I hold close to my heart.

With your support, my poetry finds its voice and my words find their wings. Thank you all for being a part of this beautiful journey

Notes on the poems

In the realm of poetic creation, there exists a unique space where inspiration weaves itself into profound verses. The verses, steeped in optimism and guided by a deep understanding of the world, are a testament to the poet's ceaseless curiosity and keen observation. The poet draws from the multifaceted tapestry of existence, where values, principles, and happiness form the backdrop of their poetic canvas. Their exploration leads them to a realization that transcends the superficial, delving into the very essence of happiness as a sense of inner bliss and a profound appreciation for the interconnectedness of all things. Moreover, the verse takes us on a journey of spiritual awakening, one not defined by legendary feats, but by the discovery of inner tranquillity and a broader, more enlightened perspective. Lastly, the poet engages in a reflection on the complexities of consciousness and humanity, offering their personal interpretation of our contemporary world. Throughout their poetic journey, clarity stands as a guiding principle, allowing readers to navigate the profound ideas with ease and resonate with the poet's quest for understanding the intricate interplay of life's elements.

let's elaborate on the insights provided by the poet regarding the creation and inspiration behind the poem:

1. Inspirational Sources: The poet's primary source of inspiration is the world around them. They are deeply observant and curious, striving to gain a profound understanding of various aspects of life. This understanding, acquired through observation and contemplation, serves as the initial spark that motivates them to put pen to paper.

2. Optimism: One of the central objectives of the poet's work is to infuse it with optimism. They want their writing to serve as a beacon of positivity and hope. This reflects a belief in the power of literature and poetry to uplift and inspire, even in the face of life's challenges.

3. Values and Principles: The poet is intrigued by the values and principles upheld by diverse individuals and communities. They seem to be on a quest to explore the moral and ethical foundations that guide people's lives. This exploration likely involves delving into different cultures, traditions, and belief systems to gain a more profound insight into the human experience.

4. Happiness: Happiness is a recurring theme in the poem. The poet acknowledges that happiness is a universal desire but recognizes that it can be experienced in highly individualized ways. Beyond the surface, they dig deeper to explore happiness as a state of profound contentment with oneself and an appreciation for the beauty and harmony in the world.

5. Spiritual Awakening: The second part of the poem delves into the idea of spiritual awakening. This awakening is not positioned as an endeavour to become a legendary figure but rather as a personal journey to discover inner peace. It leads to a broader and more profound perception of the world, suggesting that the poet values spiritual and emotional growth as an essential part of life's journey.

6. Reflection on Consciousness and Humanity: The third part of the poem involves reflection on consciousness and humanity. This indicates the poet's engagement with deep philosophical and existential questions. They may be exploring the human condition, the state of the world, and their own perspective on these matters. This introspection reveals a keen awareness of the interconnectedness of all living beings and a desire to understand and address contemporary issues.

7. Clarity: Throughout the creative process, the poet places a strong emphasis on clarity. They aim to express their thoughts and ideas in a straightforward and accessible manner. This commitment to clarity is evident in the structure and themes of their poetry, as they strive to convey their message in a way that is easily understood by a broad audience.

In summary, the poet draws inspiration from the world's diversity, values, and principles, with a focus on happiness and spiritual growth. They contemplate the human condition and the state of the world with a commitment to expressing their ideas with clarity. These insights provide a deeper understanding of the poem's themes and intentions, making it a more impactful and thought-provoking piece of literature.

Reader's guide

Navigating the Poet's Insights

The Spark of Understanding: As you venture into this collection of verses, it's important to recognize that the poet's creative process is ignited by the deep understanding of the world and its intricate nuances. Their ability to observe and comprehend the multifaceted nature of life serves as the foundation upon which the poetry is constructed. As you immerse yourself in the poet's work, consider how her keen insights and observations provide a unique lens through which to view the world.

A Beacon of Optimism: Throughout these verses, an overarching theme of optimism and hope is palpable. The poet's intention is to infuse each line with a sense of positivity that is designed to inspire and uplift. It's an opportunity for readers to explore how this pervasive optimism influences their own interpretations and perspectives on the verses, ultimately inviting a brighter outlook on life.

Values and Principles Unveiled: Central to the poet's exploration are the values and principles that underpin diverse cultures and individuals. These themes form the heartbeat of their work, offering readers the chance to reflect upon their own principles and values in light of the poet's poetic narratives. The verses encourage introspection, challenging readers to consider the values that guide their own lives.

The Many Facets of Happiness: Happiness, an aspiration shared universally, is a central thread in this collection. The poet's contemplation of happiness extends beyond the superficial, prompting readers to delve into the deeper layers of this emotion. Happiness, as portrayed in these verses, is not merely an external pursuit but a profound inner state of contentment and an appreciation for the interconnectedness of all aspects of existence.

The Journey of Spiritual Awakening: In the second part of this collection, the poet invites readers to explore the concept of spiritual awakening. It is a journey not defined by the pursuit of legendary feats but by the discovery of inner tranquillity and a broader, more enlightened perspective on the world. As you engage with this section, consider how the poet's perspective on spiritual growth resonates with your own understanding.

Reflections on Consciousness and Humanity: The third part of the collection takes readers on a profound journey through reflections on consciousness and humanity. Here, the poet's unique viewpoint offers a fresh lens through which to contemplate the human condition and the state of the world. The verses encourage readers to explore their own perspectives and engage in thoughtful reflection.

The Poetry of Clarity: Throughout this collection, clarity is a consistent thread that weaves its way through the poet's work. The commitment to clarity is not merely about elucidating complex ideas but also about enhancing the emotional resonance of the verses. It serves as a guide for readers to navigate and connect with the profound concepts explored within the poetry.

Unearthing Interconnectedness: The theme of interconnectedness subtly weaves its way throughout this collection, inviting readers to consider the poet's exploration of this concept. It encourages a deeper understanding of the interconnected nature of existence and the shared responsibility that comes with it. As you engage with these verses, contemplate how this theme may evoke your own sense of interconnectedness with the world and the responsibilities it entails.

This journey through the poet's insights is an invitation to engage with their observations, inspirations, and reflections. As you read, allow the verses to spark your own contemplations and resonate with your life experiences. Ultimately, it's an opportunity to embrace the poet's optimism, discover the depths of clarity, and explore the interconnectedness of existence in a way that resonates with your own unique journey.

Afterword

In the Echoes of Verses

As we reach the final pages of this collection, I am filled with gratitude for the incredible journey we have taken together through the tapestry of verses. Poetry possesses a rare alchemy, transforming emotions, observations, and inspirations into a tapestry of words that weaves its way into our hearts. In these pages, I have endeavoured to capture the essence of life's diverse and intricate tapestry.

My heartfelt appreciation goes out to each and every one of you, my cherished readers, who have embarked on this poetic odyssey with me. It is your presence on this journey that has given life and meaning to these verses. Poetry truly finds its wings when it resonates with the souls that embrace it, and it's with profound gratitude that I acknowledge the resonance you've brought to these words.

Throughout this collection, I have striven to offer a spectrum of themes—optimism, the exploration of values and principles, the multi-layered facets of happiness, the journey of spiritual awakening, reflections on consciousness and humanity, and the guiding beacon of clarity. It is my hope that each piece has ignited a spark, kindled contemplation, or served as a bridge for connection.

However, a collection of verses is more than mere words on a page. It represents the poet's journey and the shared voyage of both the writer and the reader. In this afterword, I wish to express my profound gratitude for the privilege of sharing this literary voyage with you. These verses have been my companions through moments of inspiration, reflection, and creative fervour. It is in these moments that I have felt most connected to you, my readers, knowing that we have shared in the universal human experience.

I wish to extend my deepest appreciation to those who have been steadfast pillars of support and a wellspring of inspiration throughout this poetic journey. To my family and friends, whose unwavering encouragement has been my cornerstone. To the poets and writers whose works have ignited the flame of my own creativity, and to the artists and thinkers who have illuminated my path.

A special thank you goes to those who have engaged in profound and thought-provoking discussions about my work. Your insights have not only enriched my understanding of the themes explored within these pages but have also added layers of depth to the poetic narrative. Your interpretations, whether in alignment or contrast with my own, have been invaluable and enlightening.

In conclusion, it is my hope that this collection of verses has not only allowed you to glimpse into my world but has also ignited a spark of introspection and exploration in your own life. I encourage you to delve into the realm of poetry, be it as a reader or a creator, for within its verses, you may discover echoes of your own journey and the profound beauty inherent in the written word.

Thank you for being a part of this shared literary journey, and may the echoes of these verses reverberate within your hearts long after the final page is turned.

With heartfelt gratitude,
Ciju Jonathan

Dedication

To all the cherished readers of these poems

Printed in Great Britain
by Amazon

33139427R00078